20 Marvelous Math Tales

Fun, Reproducible Stories With Companion Word Problems That Build Important Math Skills...and Promote Literacy!

by Betsy Franco

SCHOLASTIC
PROFESSIONAL BOOKS

New York • Toronto • London • Auckland • Sydney • Mexico City • New Delhi • Hong Kong

Dedication

For Lill and Lottie,
who had lots of stories to tell

Cover design by Norma Ortiz

Cover illustration by Anne Kennedy

Interior design by Ellen Matlach Hassell
for Boultinghouse & Boultinghouse, Inc.

Interior illustration by Maxie Chambliss

ISBN: 0-439-15393-X

Printed in the U.S.A.

Contents

Introduction

20 Marvelous Math Tales is a collection of short stories that builds early problem-solving skills while developing reading comprehension. The stories are fun, engaging, and mathematically rich. Following each story are related problems for students to solve. They will meet Mr. Pig and his amazing machine, help Red Riding Hood save endangered animals, solve Ronny's riddles, and much more.

Benefits of Using the Book

The major benefits of using the problem-solving stories in this book include the following:

- The humor and subject matter of the stories engage students in the problem-solving process.

- Students learn and practice specific early problem-solving strategies one at a time.

- Students add some powerful problem-solving strategies to their "tool boxes."

- Students practice a wide variety of math skills in the context of problem solving.

- The stories help build students' reading comprehension skills.

Problem-Solving Strategies

The book is organized into seven sections. The stories in each section focus on a specific problem-solving strategy. The beginning of each section includes a simple introduction to the strategy that uses an entertaining example for students. A list of the problem-solving strategies appears below.

> Understanding the Problem
> Guess and Check
> Use Objects/Make a Model
> Draw a Picture/Draw a Graph
> Find a Pattern
> Make a Table/Make an Organized List
> Use Logical Reasoning

Of course, students may combine strategies or choose to draw a picture in the "Find a Pattern" section. As long as they're thinking, problem solving works!

Math Skills

While engaging in the problem-solving process, students will gain practice in the following math skills:

Addition
Subtraction
Multiplication
Division
Place Value
Number Sense
Fractions
Geometry
Time
Money
Graphing
Measurement
Patterns
Discrete Math
Logical Reasoning

How to Use the Book

This book can be used in a variety of ways. It is helpful to present the strategy for each section before introducing the stories in that section. Once the strategy has been introduced and discussed, you can read the story to the class, or photocopy it for students.

Students can work individually or in pairs or groups to solve the problems related to the story. Working together can be beneficial because students learn from and are inspired by each other's ideas. In the same vein, it can be helpful for the whole class to discuss the answers and strategies at the end of the lesson.

Answers for the problems appear at the back of the book.

Introducing the Strategy:

Understanding the Problem

Story problems are easier to solve if you work them out step by step. You can be a successful problem solver if you make sure you understand what the problem is asking, find the information you need to solve it, and decide what you need to do to solve it. Read the example story below.

Sam Snail was tired of moving so slowly. He decided to buy himself a tiny skateboard for $0.57 and a tiny helmet and kneepads for $0.38. Before Sam went to the counter to pay, he wondered how much he would have to pay in all. He had a one-dollar bill in his pocket. Sam wondered how much money he would have left.

To help Sam answer his questions, you can solve the problem step by step.

1. **What does Sam want to know?** He wants to know how much he will pay in all.

2. **What information do you need to solve the problem?** The skateboard costs $0.57, and the helmet and kneepads cost $0.38.

3. **What do you need to do to solve the problem?** The words *How much* and *in all* are clues. They tell you that you need to add.

$$\begin{array}{r} \$0.57 \\ +\ 0.38 \\ \hline \$0.95 \end{array}$$

4. **What else does Sam want to know?** He wants to know how much money he will have left.

5. **What information do you need to solve the problem?** Sam has a one-dollar bill. The items cost $0.95.

6. **What do you need to do to solve the problem?** The words *how much* and *left* are clues. They tell you that you should subtract.

$$\$1.00 - \$0.95 = \$0.05$$

23　7　36　11　8　4　19　25　10　4　17　2　33　42　16　9　5　20　3　31

The Wild Animal Picnic

Dove was always trying to think of ways to make the wild animals friendlier to each other. He decided to have a picnic for everyone.

"You won't catch me at a picnic with Lion," declared Zebra. "He eats too much."

"I'd be afraid that Lion would eat me," said Monkey.

"Me, too," added Mouse. "He's always looking at me and licking his lips."

Dove thought. Then he said, "If we all bring plenty of food, then no one will be hungry. No one will need to be afraid, and we can all have a picnic together!"

That made sense to the animals—even Mouse. The elephants, giraffes, and zebras brought salad. The monkeys brought bananas. The lions brought sandwiches. The mice brought berries. Even the bees came and brought honey, of course.

After the picnic, the crickets played music, and the frog-and-toad chorus sang with the coyotes. The ants washed all the dishes and put them away. Everyone had a wonderful time.

Dove was very happy and announced that there would be a wild animal picnic once a year from then on.

20 Marvelous Math Tales　Scholastic Professional Books

The Wild Animal Picnic

**To get an idea of what happened at the picnic, read each question.
Circle the information you need to answer the question.
Underline the question.
Then find the answer.
The first one is done for you.**

1. The elephants brought (37 pounds) of leaves for the salad. The zebras and giraffes brought (46 pounds) of leaves. <u>How many more pounds of leaves did the zebras and giraffes bring than the elephants?</u>

   Answer: <u>9 pounds of leaves</u>

2. All the wild cats came to the picnic. There were 17 lions, 18 leopards, and 9 jaguars. How many wild cats came to the picnic in all?

   Answer: _____

3. A total of 23 zebras were at the picnic. Of those, 16 zebras played kickball. The rest of the zebras played horseshoes. How many zebras played horseshoes?

   Answer: _____

4. All the rodents—all the mice and rats—had a great time at the picnic. There were 55 mice and 49 rats at the picnic. How many rodents were there all together?

   Answer: _____

5. There was a banana-eating contest at the picnic. There were 3 monkeys. Each monkey ate 9 bananas. How many bananas did they eat in all?

   Answer: _____

6. Dove invited 59 bees and 76 wasps to the picnic. All of them came. How many more wasps came to the picnic than bees?

   Answer: _____

7. The lions ate 132 sandwiches from one plate and 49 sandwiches from another plate. How many sandwiches did the lions eat in all?

   Answer: _____

8. The frog-and-toad chorus had 145 frogs and 98 toads. What was the total number of frogs and toads in the chorus?

   Answer: _____

Froggy's Day at the Store

Froggy had made her bed. She had swept the kitchen floor. She had taken out the garbage.

"Here's your allowance, Froggy," her mother said. "You've done all your chores this week. Here's 55¢ for you to save or spend."

"Thanks, Mom," replied Froggy. She put the money in her coin purse. Then she hopped across the pond to the Amphibian and Reptile Store.

The store had so many wonderful things to buy. There were spiders. There were boxes filled with gnats. Flies were on sale—only 24¢ each. Froggy saw worms and different sizes of crickets.

Her mouth watering, Froggy took the money out of her coin purse. She didn't want to spend every penny of the 55¢. She wanted to have a little left over to save in her piggy bank.

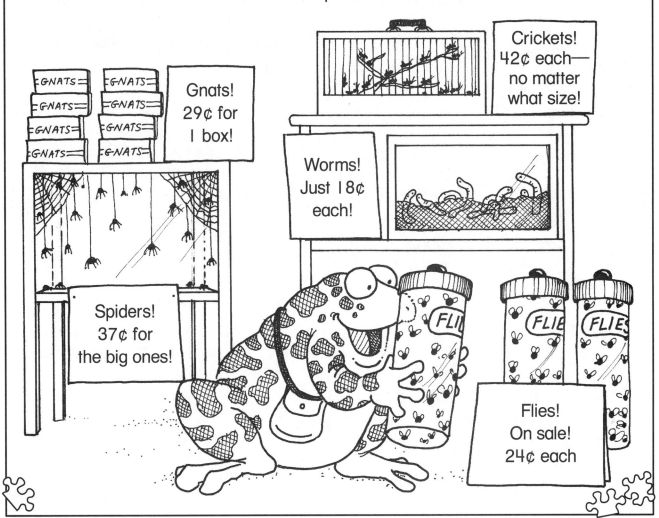

Gnats! 29¢ for 1 box!

Crickets! 42¢ each— no matter what size!

Worms! Just 18¢ each!

Spiders! 37¢ for the big ones!

Flies! On sale! 24¢ each

20 Marvelous Math Tales Scholastic Professional Books

Froggy's Day at the Store

For each problem, decide whether to add or subtract.
Then write your answer.
The first one is done for you.

1. How much more do the crickets cost than the spiders?

   I will **subtract**_____.

   Answer: 5¢ _____

2. How much would it cost to buy 1 spider and 1 worm?

   I will _____.

   Answer: _____

   Why wouldn't Froggy buy 1 spider and 1 worm?

   _____

3. How much do 2 boxes of gnats cost?

   I will _____.

   Answer: _____

4. How much more money does Froggy need to buy 2 boxes of gnats?

   I will _____.

   Answer: _____

5. How much would it cost to buy 2 worms and 1 cricket?

   I will _____.

   Answer: _____

6. How much do 3 worms cost?

   I will _____.

   Answer: _____

7. How much will Froggy have left over if she buys 3 worms?

   I will _____.

   Answer: _____

8. What would you buy at the Amphibian and Reptile Store if you were Froggy? (Remember, she doesn't want to spend all her money.)

   Answer: _____

   How much would the items cost?

   _____

Red Riding Hood and the Gray Wolf

Little Red Riding Hood loved to visit her grandmother. She always brought fruit from her garden to her grandmother. Red Riding Hood and her grandmother would talk about ways to help Earth. One day, when Red Riding Hood was going through the woods to see her grandmother, she saw lots of interesting animals. A garter snake slithered along beside her. A bald eagle flew over her head. She even saw a condor with large wings perched in a tree.

"All of these animals are endangered," Red Riding Hood said to herself. "Grandma and I must do something to help them."

When she got to Grandma's house, another guest had arrived. Sitting close to Grandma was a real gray wolf.

"My, what a surprise!" exclaimed Red Riding Hood. She looked at her grandmother. "Are you okay?"

"Well, not really," Grandma answered. "Wolf and I have been talking. He's been endangered for such a long time."

"We wolves are doing better than we have been," Wolf added. "But we must keep working to save wolves and other animals."

"We want to make 'Save the Wolf' posters to put up at city hall," Grandma said. "But I don't have any markers or cardboard."

"I've got lots of markers and some cardboard at home," Red Riding Hood volunteered. "I'll just run home and get them."

Wolf knew the woods well. He showed Red Riding Hood a map. There were three different paths she could take to get back home.

20 Marvelous Math Tales Scholastic Professional Books

Red Riding Hood and the Gray Wolf

Look at Wolf's map on page 14. Find the shortest way from Grandma's house to Red Riding Hood's house. Work out the problem step by step. Cut out the centimeter ruler at the side of the map. Use it to measure the distances.

1. First look at the path that goes by the big rock. Measure the three distances on the path (from dot to dot) and write the lengths on the map. Add the three lengths. How long is the path?

_____

2. Next find the length of the path that goes by the tallest tree. Measure and add the three distances. How long is that path?

_____

3. Finally look at the path that goes by the cave. Measure and add the three distances. How long is that path?

_____

4. Compare the three paths. Which path do you think Red Riding Hood should take? Tell why.

_____

_____

   After returning to Grandma's house, Red Riding Hood, Grandma, and Wolf made posters. Then Wolf pulled out a map to figure out the best way to City Hall. Look at the map on page 15.

5. How long is the path that goes by the Fire Station?

_____

6. How long is the path that goes by the Library?

_____

7. Which path should they take to City Hall and why?

_____

_____

_____

Name _____

Map to Grandma's House

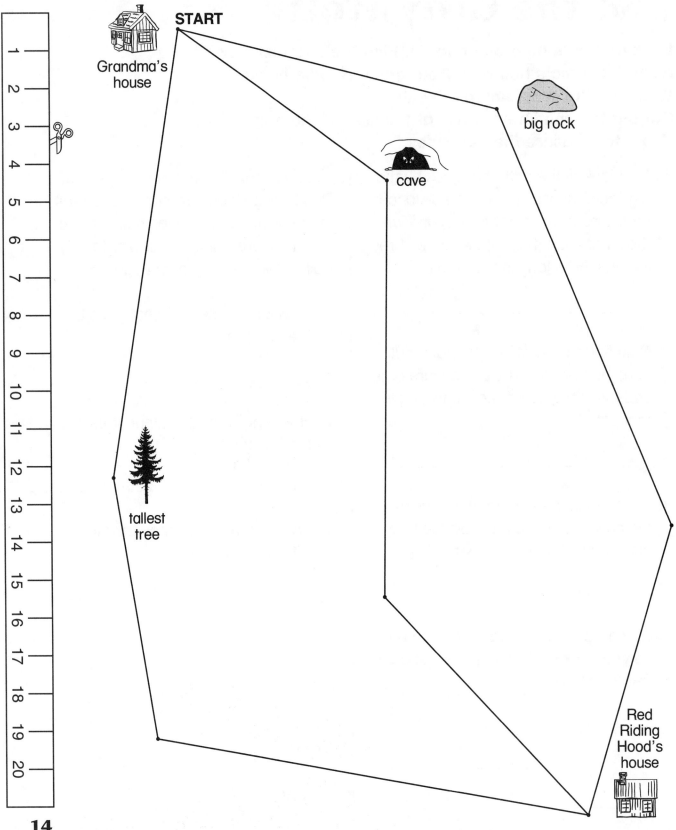

START

Grandma's house

big rock

cave

tallest tree

Red Riding Hood's house

1 2 3 4 5 6 7 8 9 10 11 12 13 14 15 16 17 18 19 20

14

23 · 7 · 36 · 11 · 8 · 4 · 19 · 25 · 10 · 4 · 17 · 2 · 33 · 42 · 16 · 9 · 5 · 20 · 3 · 31

Map to City Hall

START

Grandma's house

Fire Station

Library

City Hall

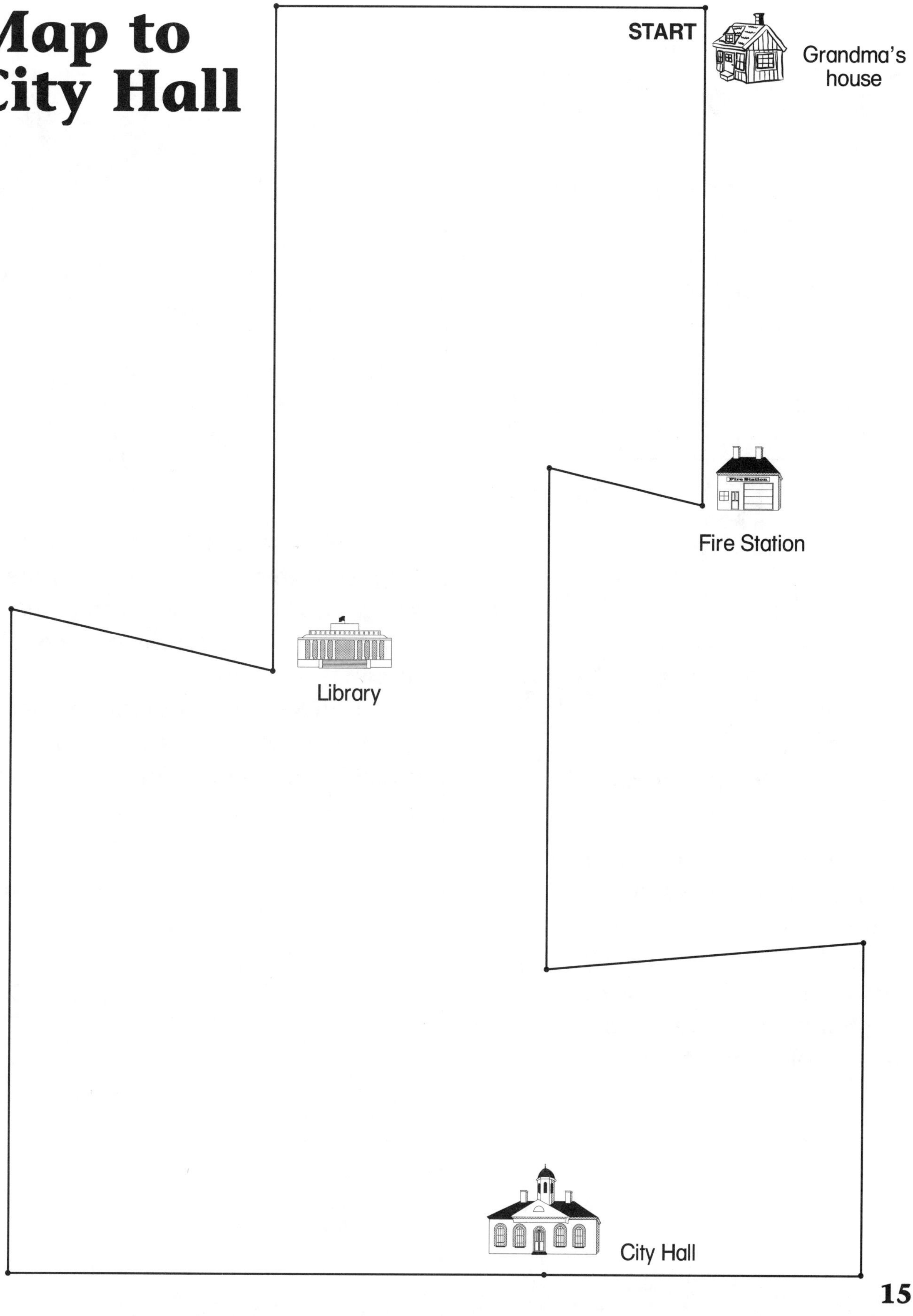

Introducing the Strategy:
Guess and Check

Sometimes the best way to solve a problem is to make reasonable guesses and then check to see if they work. The example below shows how the Guess and Check strategy works.

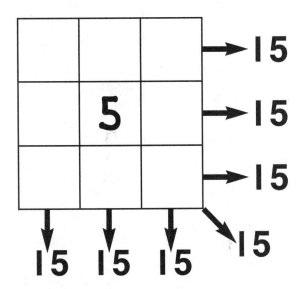

Use the numbers 1–9.

Sarah was trying to fill in a magic square. In the magic square, the sum of three squares always had to be 15. It didn't matter if she added across, up and down, or diagonally. Sarah sat and stared at the magic square for a long time.

Finally she said, "I'm just going to guess which numbers go in the squares. I'm going to write some numbers in the squares and check to see if they work."

Sarah kept writing numbers in the squares in different ways and checking the sums. On her sixth try, all the sums checked out!

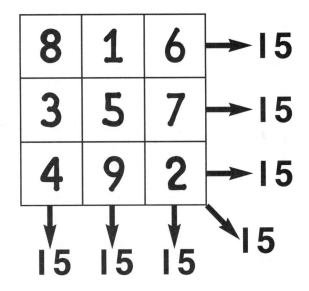

16

23 7 36 11 8 4 19 25 10 4 17 2 33 4 16 9 5 20 3 31

Ms. Squid and the Homework Mess

Ms. Squid had a habit of doing too much at one time. This caused a lot of trouble for the fish in her class. She would read a book, pass out math tests, and do a science experiment all at the same time. If someone interrupted Ms. Squid, she would get upset. Then she would spray ink everywhere!

That's what happened on Tuesday. Ms. Squid was handing out the math homework. Just then, a tiger shark swam by the window.

"Shark!" screamed Andy Angelfish.

Ms. Squid's glasses fell off. She dropped everything and squirted black ink all over the homework.

"Hey, we can't do our homework now!" Bill Butterfly Fish shouted.

"Oh, yes, you can," Ms. Squid said. "In fact, I'll give you the answer sheet. It has ink all over it, too. All you have to do is fill in the numbers that are covered by the ink."

Ms. Squid and the Homework Mess

Look at Ms. Squid's answer sheet below. Use the guess and check strategy to fill in the missing numbers. Write each number inside the ink spot.

Addition

1.
```
   2 5
 + 5 ◯
 ─────
   7 8
```

2.
```
   4 ◯
 + ◯ 2
 ─────
   7 9
```

3.
```
   ◯ 4
 + 1 ◯
 ─────
   6 8
```

4.
```
   4 5
 + ◯ 8
 ─────
   8 3
```

5.
```
   ◯ 2
 + 7 9
 ─────
   9 1
```

6.
```
   3 5
 + 2 ◯
 ─────
   6 2
```

Subtraction

7.
```
   9 5
 - 3 ◯
 ─────
   6 3
```

8.
```
   6 8
 - ◯ ◯
 ─────
   4 2
```

9.
```
   7 ◯
 - ◯ 2
 ─────
   3 7
```

10.
```
   ◯ ◯
 - 4 5
 ─────
   4 3
```

11.
```
   8 6
 - ◯ 7
 ─────
   2 9
```

12.
```
   ◯ 4
 - 6 7
 ─────
   1 7
```

20 Marvelous Math Tales   Scholastic Professional Books

Benny's Contests

Benny loves contests. He enters contests about who can speak the loudest or who can nap the longest. Benny loves school, too. He loves Mondays because there is an estimating jar. He loves Fridays because there is always a spelling bee. Benny's favorite place in the classroom is the math center because it has games to play and problems to solve.

One day, Mr. Moss, the teacher, put the following problem in the math center:

Put the numbers in the boxes. Find the biggest difference you can.

4 5 6 7

```
   ☐  ☐
-  ☐  ☐
  ─────
```

Benny's answer looked like this:

```
   7  6
-  5  4
  ─────
   2  2
```

Hallie went to the center and worked on the puzzle, too. She got a greater difference than Benny did. Everyone looked to see if Benny would be upset. But he surprised them all.

"That's okay," he smiled. "I don't have to win every contest. I just like to solve problems. Let's keep playing!"

Name _____

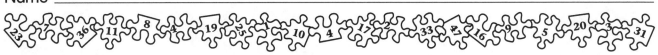

Benny's Contests

1. Show how Hallie got a greater difference than Benny did.

   4 5 6 7

2. The next day Mr. Moss put this problem in the math center. He told the students to use the numbers to find the greatest difference.

   2 3 7 8

Here's how Benny solved it. Write Benny's difference.

7	8

2 3 7 8

−	3	2

3. Can you get a greater difference than Benny did?

   2 3 7 8

4. What is the greatest difference you can get using these numbers?

   2 4 6 9

5. What is the least difference you can get using these numbers?

   2 4 6 9

6. What are the greatest and the least differences you can get using these numbers?

Greatest

   5 6 7 9

Least

   5 6 7 9

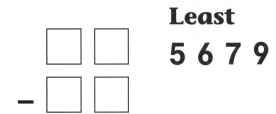

20 Marvelous Math Tales   Scholastic Professional Books

Jenny's Goofy Calculator

Whenever something broke in Jenny's house, she was the one who fixed it. She loved to take things apart and put them together again. She had fixed the screen door and the basketball hoop.

Jenny also loved to look inside things and see how they worked. She had looked inside the computer, the telephone, the answering machine, and the alarm clock. One day Jenny took apart the calculator and fiddled with it. When she put it back together, the calculator acted very goofy. Only seven of the keys worked. The $+$, $-$, and $=$ keys and the number keys 2, 3, 6, and 7 were the only keys that would work.

Jenny took this as a challenge. She decided to try to make all the numbers from 1 to 100 on her goofy calculator. Here's how Jenny made some of the numbers. Try them on your calculator.

$$7 - 6 = \boxed{1}$$

$$2 = \boxed{2}$$

$$7 + 3 = \boxed{10}$$

$$2\,3 - 6 = \boxed{17}$$

$$3\,2 - 7 = \boxed{25}$$

$$6\,2 + 3 = \boxed{65}$$

Jenny's Goofy Calculator

Use your calculator to help Jenny make some of the larger numbers. Remember you can use only the following keys:

$+$ $-$ $=$ 2 3 6 7

You may use each key more than once.

Write a number in each blank calculator key below.

1. ☐ ☐ $+$ 7 $=$ | 40

2. ☐ ☐ $-$ 3 $=$ | 19

3. ☐ ☐ $+$ 6 $=$ | 68

4. 6 3 $-$ ☐ $=$ | 56

5. 2 7 $+$ ☐ $=$ | 59

6. ☐ ☐ $-$ 3 $=$ | 29

7. ☐ ☐ $+$ 7 3 $=$ | 100

8. 6 7 $-$ ☐ ☐ $=$ | 44

9. 7 2 $-$ ☐ ☐ $=$ | 45

10. ☐ ☐ $-$ ☐ ☐ $=$ | 35

20 Marvelous Math Tales   Scholastic Professional Books

Puzzle Mania

Skye's parents always knew what to get their daughter for her birthday. Skye had a "thing" about puzzles. She finished at least one crossword puzzle every day. Her jigsaw puzzles covered the entire living room floor. Skye liked math puzzles, word puzzles, brain twisters, and any other kinds of puzzles she could get her hands on.

But Skye had a problem. Every day after school she worked at her mother's store. Skye didn't like her job very much because she couldn't solve puzzles at the store.

Then one day she had an idea.

Skye said to Mrs. Baker, the next customer, "The pencil you want to buy costs 30¢. Tell me how many coins you have that total 30¢. Don't show them to me. Let me guess what the coins are."

"I have 5 coins," Mrs. Baker answered.

"Five coins. Let me think." Skye tapped her chin. "You have 4 nickels and 1 dime. That's 30¢."

"That's right!" Mrs. Baker cried. "How did you do that?"

From that day on, Skye loved working at the store. She solved puzzles all afternoon by guessing what kinds of coins everyone had. Then she would go home to her jigsaw puzzles and her crossword puzzles. And when she grew up . . . Skye became a top-notch detective.

Puzzle Mania

Solve some of Skye's puzzles.
Tell which coins the customers had.
Write a number from 0 to 9 in each blank.

1. Mrs. Bole bought stickers for 30¢. She paid with 5 coins.

   She had _____ quarters, _____ dimes,

   _____ nickels, _____ pennies.

2. Mr. Wheat bought a key chain for 57¢. He paid with 6 coins.

   He had _____ quarters, _____ dimes,

   _____ nickels, _____ pennies.

3. Sam bought a box of crayons for 81¢. He paid with 5 coins.

   He had _____ quarters, _____ dimes,

   _____ nickels, _____ pennies.

4. Nell Bright bought a small flashlight for $1.25. She paid with 5 coins.

   She had _____ quarters, _____ dimes,

   _____ nickels, _____ pennies.

5. Ms. Redding bought red ribbon for 45¢. She paid with 9 coins.

   She had _____ quarters, _____ dimes,

   _____ nickels, _____ pennies.

6. Tim bought a balsa wood airplane for 77¢. He used the least number of coins he could.

   He had _____ quarters, _____ dimes,

   _____ nickels, _____ pennies.

7. Bo bought a yo-yo for 99¢. He used the least number of coins possible.

   He had _____ quarters, _____ dimes,

   _____ nickels, _____ pennies.

8. Sammy bought some licorice whips for 84¢. She used the least number of coins possible.

   She had _____ quarters, _____ dimes,

   _____ nickels, _____ pennies.

24

20 Marvelous Math Tales   Scholastic Professional Books

Introducing the Strategies:
Use Objects
Make a Model

It's easier to find the solutions to some problems if you use real objects that you can hold and move around, or if you make a model of the problem. Look at the example below.

Mark made 16 brownies for the bake sale. He wanted to put them on plates. But Mark liked everything to work out nice and evenly. So, of course, he wanted each plate to have the same number of brownies.

If Mark uses 2 plates, will each plate have the same number of brownies? What if he uses 3 plates, 4 plates, or 5 plates?

Gather 16 cubes or other objects (for the brownies) and 5 pieces of paper (for the plates). Try putting the cubes on 2 plates, 3 plates, and so on.

You'll find that if Mark uses 2 plates or 4 plates, each plate will have the same number of brownies.

2 plates:

4 plates:

Bumblebee Gets Curious

Bumblebee had lived with hexagons his whole life. He knew a hexagon had 6 sides. He knew a hexagon had 6 corners. He knew that if he drew a line down the middle of a hexagon, it would make two matching parts. That means he knew a hexagon was **symmetrical**.

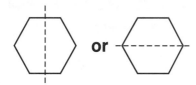 **or**

Bumblebee knew hexagons were good for storing honey. The shapes fit together side by side by side inside his hive.

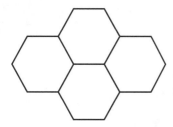

Bumble was a curious bee. He wondered about other shapes, too. "What about squares, rectangles, triangles, pentagons, and octagons?" he thought.

So, Bumble decided to explore the other shapes. After all, maybe one of them might be a better shape for the hive.

20 Marvelous Math Tales Scholastic Professional Books

Bumblebee Gets Curious

Help Bumble explore the other shapes.
Cut out the shapes on page 29 and
use them to answer the problems.

Square

1. A square has _____ sides.

2. A square has _____ corners.

3. Can you fold a square in half to make
two matching parts? _____

Triangle 1

7. Triangle 1 has _____ sides.

8. Triangle 1 has _____ corners.

9. Can you fold this triangle in half to
make two matching parts? _____

Rectangle

4. A rectangle has _____ sides.

5. A rectangle has _____ corners.

6. Can you fold a rectangle in half to
make two matching parts? _____

Triangle 2

10. Triangle 2 has _____ sides.

11. Triangle 2 has _____ corners.

12. Can you fold this triangle in half to
make two matching parts? _____

Bumblebee Gets Curious

Pentagon

13. A pentagon has _____ sides.

14. A pentagon has _____ corners.

15. Can you fold this pentagon in half to

   make two matching parts? _____

Octagon

16. An octagon has _____ sides.

17. An octagon has _____ corners.

18. Can you fold this octagon in half to

   make two matching parts? _____

19. What do you notice about the number of sides and the number of corners on each shape?

   _____

   _____

20. Trace and cut out 3 more copies of each shape. You should have 4 of each shape. Which of the same shapes fit side by side without any space in between them or without overlapping?

   _____

   _____

   _____

   Which of the same shapes don't fit side by side?

   _____

   _____

   _____

   Bumble worked all day comparing the shapes. At the end of the day, he decided that the hexagon was the best shape for the hive after all. It had lots of corners and sides, it was symmetrical, and hexagons fit side by side by side!

20 Marvelous Math Tales   Scholastic Professional Books

Shapes

square

rectangle

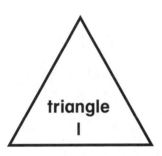

triangle
1

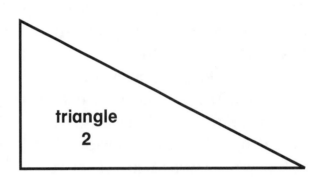

triangle
2

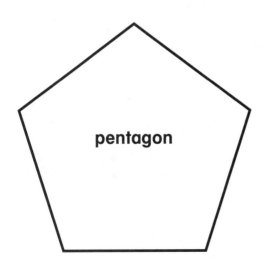

pentagon

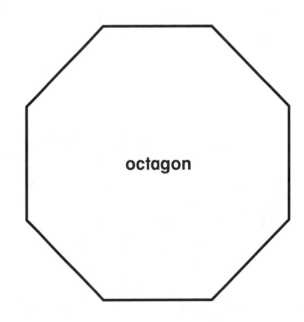

octagon

Squirrel's Acorn Problem

Every summer Squirrel hid his acorns in the ground for the long winter. He would spend months finding the very best acorns and hiding them near the tree he lived in. But when winter came, Squirrel couldn't remember where he had hidden all his acorns. As he looked for them, he dug up practically all the dirt around his tree. It was very annoying.

One winter, Squirrel had an idea for solving his winter problem. He asked Spider to spin a giant grid on the ground. The grid had 100 squares in it. Then Squirrel had Spider spin a number in each square of the grid.

That winter, when Squirrel hid his acorns, he wrote himself directions. The directions were in a special code so no one else could find the hidden acorns.

One of Squirrel's directions read, "Start on 24. Add 10. Subtract 4."

Squirrel tested his directions.

✔ He started on 24.

✔ He added 10 by jumping down to 34.

✔ He subtracted 4 by jumping back 4 spaces.

✔ He landed on 30.

When Squirrel dug under the number 30, sure enough, he found an acorn there!

1	2	3	4	5	6	7	8	9	10
11	12	13	14	15	16	17	18	19	20
21	22	23	24	25	26	27	28	29	30
31	32	33	34	35	36	37	38	39	40
41	42	43	44	45	46	47	48	49	50
51	52	53	54	55	56	57	58	59	60
61	62	63	64	65	66	67	68	69	70
71	72	73	74	75	76	77	78	79	80
81	82	83	84	85	86	87	88	89	90
91	92	93	94	95	96	97	98	99	100

20 Marvelous Math Tales   Scholastic Professional Books

Squirrel's Acorn Problem

When winter came, Squirrel knew exactly where his acorns were. Help him find some of them by following his directions. Use a cube or counter. Move it around the hundred chart on page 33. Write the number of the square where the acorn is.

1. Start on 37.
Subtract 20.
Add 2.
The acorn is on _____ .

2. Start on 65.
Add 20.
Subtract 4.
The acorn is on _____ .

3. Start on 14.
Add 10.
Add 4.
Subtract 20.
The acorn is on _____ .

4. Start on 77.
Subtract 50.
Subtract 5.
The acorn is on _____ .

5. Start on 54.
Add 30.
Add 8.
The acorn is on _____ .

(Hint: When you get to 90, keep going to 91.)

6. Start on 27.
Add 20.
Add 6.
The acorn is on _____ .

7. Start on 33.
Subtract 10.
Subtract 3.
The acorn is on _____ .

8. Start on 88.
Subtract 30.
Subtract 9.
The acorn is on _____ .

Squirrel's Acorn Problem

Some of Squirrel's directions were shorter. For example,
one of his directions read, "Start at 68. Subtract 24."
To subtract 24, Squirrel would jump up 20 and land on 48.
Then he would move back 4 spaces and land on 44.
Try it on the hundred chart. Then find the rest of the acorns.

9. Start at 53.
Subtract 31.
The acorn is on _____.

10. Start at 26.
Add 45.
The acorn is on _____.

11. Start at 100.
Subtract 58.
The acorn is on _____.

12. Start at 23.
Add 67.
The acorn is on _____.

13. Start at 17.
Add 71.
Subtract 21.
The acorn is on _____.

14. Start at 84.
Subtract 53.
Add 38.
The acorn is on _____.

15. Start at 50.
Add 11.
The acorn is on _____.

16. Start at 47.
Add 45.
The acorn is on _____.

17. Start at 42.
Subtract 23.
The acorn is on _____.

18. Start at 74.
Subtract 45.
The acorn is on _____.

20 Marvelous Math Tales   Scholastic Professional Books

Hundred Chart

1	2	3	4	5	6	7	8	9	10
11	12	13	14	15	16	17	18	19	20
21	22	23	24	25	26	27	28	29	30
31	32	33	34	35	36	37	38	39	40
41	42	43	44	45	46	47	48	49	50
51	52	53	54	55	56	57	58	59	60
61	62	63	64	65	66	67	68	69	70
71	72	73	74	75	76	77	78	79	80
81	82	83	84	85	86	87	88	89	90
91	92	93	94	95	96	97	98	99	100

Raccoon Makes a Quilt

Raccoon and Snake were best friends. Raccoon was very good with his hands. He loved to knit and sew quilts. Snake was cold-blooded so she was always thinking about the weather.

"Can you make me a quilt?" Snake asked one day. "Then I won't have to worry so much about the temperature."

Raccoon was delighted to help his friend Snake. He cut out 12 beautiful squares for the quilt. But then came the hard part. Raccoon had to decide how to sew the squares together. "I could make 2 rows," he thought. "I could put 6 squares in each row. Two times 6 is 12."

2 x 6 = 12

There were other ways to sew it together, too. Meanwhile, Snake was getting cold.

"It will take me a little time to find all the ways to make your quilt, Snake," said Raccoon.

"How many ways can you put 12 squares together?" Snake asked.

"You'd be surprised," Raccoon sighed.

"Okay, Raccoon," said Snake, "but the days are getting shorter. Please finish my quilt soon."

"Do you like to stretch out when you sleep?" Raccoon asked. "Or do you like to curl up?"

Snake rolled her eyes. "Curl up. What difference does it make?"

20 Marvelous Math Tales   Scholastic Professional Books

Raccoon Makes a Quilt

Help Raccoon make a quilt from 12 squares.

1. Cut out the 12 squares at the bottom of the page.
   Find every way to use all 12 squares to make a quilt.
   Draw each quilt below. Write a number sentence inside each quilt.

Which quilt do you think is best for Snake? Explain why.

_____

_____

Raccoon Makes a Quilt

2. How many ways can Raccoon make a quilt with 24 squares?
Use 12 squares from page 35 and cut out the 12 squares below.
Draw every way to make a quilt out of 24 squares.
(You won't be able to draw 1 x 24.)
Write a number sentence inside each quilt.

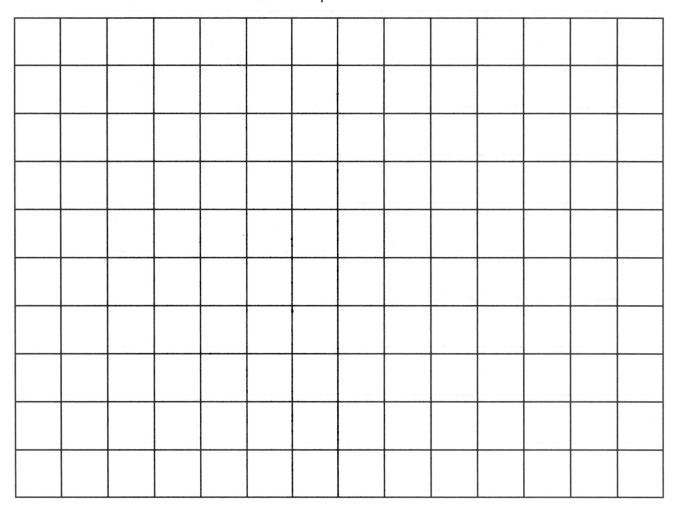

Which quilt do you think is best for Snake? Explain why.

_____

_____

20 Marvelous Math Tales   Scholastic Professional Books

What If . . . ?

Ken's favorite thing to say was "What if . . . ?" He wondered things like "What if it rains on my birthday?" and "What if a storm blows away the bakery?"

Ken's mother said it was best to wait and see what happened. She told her son, "Everything always works out."

When it was time to plan his birthday party, Ken decided to invite 6 friends. He bought 6 yo-yos as party favors. Then Ken started asking "What if . . . ?"

"What if we invite 6 friends, and we have 6 favors. If everyone comes, each person will get 1 favor," he said.

"But what if only 5 friends come? Then each friend will get 1 favor, and there will be 1 left over." He thought some more.

"What if 4 friends come? Then each friend will get 1 favor, and there will be 2 left over," Ken said.

"What if 3 friends come? Then each will get 2 favors, and there will be none left over."

He thought some more. "What if 2 friends come? Then each will get 3 favors, and there will be none left over," Ken said.

"What if only 1 friend comes? Then that friend will get 6 favors, and there will be none left over."

Finally Ken's mom said, "Let's wait and see. It will all work out!"

What If . . . ?

Ken wondered about the cake and the balloons, too.
Help him solve his "What ifs?"

There are 12 pieces of cake at the party. Each friend
will have the same number of pieces. Cut out and use
the pieces of cake on page 40 to find the answers.

1. What if 6 friends come to the party?
How many pieces of cake will each
friend get?

_____

How many pieces will be left over?

_____

2. What if 5 friends come to the party?
How many pieces of cake will each
friend get?

_____

How many pieces will be left over?

_____

3. What if 4 friends come to the party?
How many pieces of cake will each
friend get?

_____

How many pieces will be left over?

_____

4. What if 3 friends come to the party?
How many pieces of cake will each
friend get?

_____

How many pieces will be left over?

_____

5. What if 2 friends come to the party?
How many pieces of cake will each
friend get?

_____

How many pieces will be left over?

_____

6. What if 1 friend comes to the party?
How many pieces of cake will that
friend get?

_____

How many pieces will be left over?

_____

What If . . . ?

There are 18 balloons at the party. Each friend will have the same number of balloons. Cut out and use the balloons on page 40 to find the answers.

7. What if 6 friends come to the party? How many balloons will each friend get?

_____

How many balloons will be left over?

_____

8. What if 5 friends come to the party? How many balloons will each friend get?

_____

How many balloons will be left over?

_____

9. What if 4 friends come to the party? How many balloons will each friend get?

_____

How many balloons will be left over?

_____

10. What if 3 friends come to the party? How many balloons will each friend get?

_____

How many balloons will be left over?

_____

11. What if 2 friends come to the party? How many balloons will each friend get?

_____

How many balloons will be left over?

_____

12. What if 1 friend comes to the party? How many balloons will that friend get?

_____

How many balloons will be left over?

_____

At the end of the party Ken was happy. He said, "Five friends came and everything worked out anyway. Everything always works out!"

And he never said "What if" again.

23 36 11 8 4 19 25 10 4 17 33 4 16 9 5 20 3 31

Cakes and Balloons

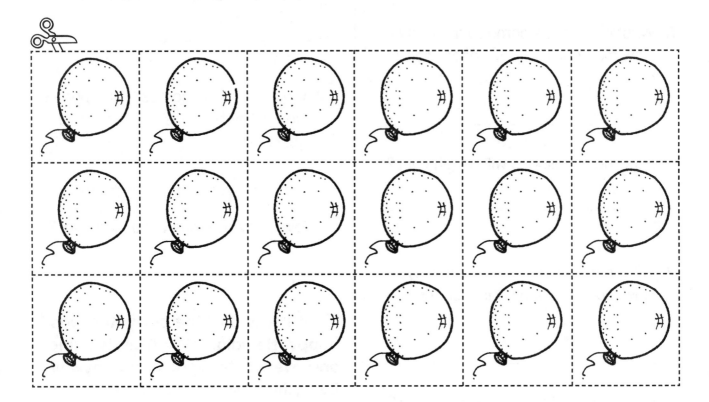

20 Marvelous Math Tales   Scholastic Professional Books

Name _____

Introducing the Strategies:

Draw a Picture
Draw a Graph

Drawing a picture or drawing a graph can help you solve many story problems. Seeing the problem on paper makes all the difference. The examples below show how these strategies work.

Draw a Picture

Jake's family owned a farm with 2-legged ostriches and 4-legged goats. One foggy day, some animals got loose. Jake could see 10 legs at the top of the hill and the tops of 4 heads, but he couldn't tell which animals were up there.

Jake started drawing pictures to figure out which animals were on the hill. He drew 2 goats and 1 ostrich. But that wasn't right. His picture had 10 legs but only 3 animals (and he needed 4 animals).

Then Jake drew 1 goat and 3 ostriches.
That worked! Jake had drawn 10 legs and 4 animals!

Draw a Graph

Jake's family also had llamas and emus on their farm. One of Jake's jobs was to count and record the number of animals. He tried counting on his fingers, but he didn't have enough fingers for all the animals. Then Jake tried remembering how many of each animal he had counted, but he got all the numbers mixed up. Finally Jake make tally marks for each animal. "What's the best way to show that there are 10 ostriches, 8 goats, 9 llamas, and 4 emus?" he asked himself. "Why don't you draw a bar graph?" his sister Dana asked. And Jake did.

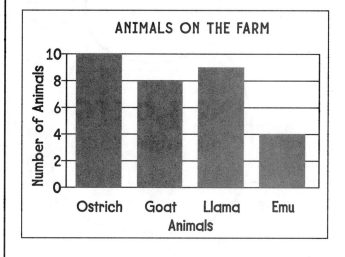

Building Snow People

Tina and Kimiko were best friends. Kimiko had just moved from Japan. Tina and Kimiko liked to compare. There were many things they did alike, and there were many things they did differently. Kimiko's favorite food was rice. There was always rice cooking in her house. Tina's favorite food was potatoes. Kimiko had books with stories like "The Peach Boy." Tina had books with stories like "Goldilocks and the Three Bears."

Then one day Tina and Kimiko built snow people. They rolled lots of snowballs of different sizes. Then they started making the snow people. Tina looked over at Kimiko's snow girl.

"Hey, Kimiko, you need another snowball to make your snow girl," said Tina.

"No, I don't," Kimiko answered. "I use 2 snowballs for a snow person. How many do you use?"

"I use 3!" said Tina.

"Well, there's another fun thing we do differently!" Kimiko said.

20 Marvelous Math Tales   Scholastic Professional Books

Building Snow People

Tina makes snow people out of 3 balls of snow. Kimiko uses 2 balls of snow. Each girl builds her own snow people. On a separate piece of paper, draw pictures to show your answers to the questions. The first one is done for you.

1. Tina and Kimiko used a total of 5 balls of snow. What did each girl's snow person look like?

Tina's   **Kimiko's**

2. They rolled and used a total of 7 balls of snow. What did their snow people look like?

3. Then Tina and Kimiko used a total of 9 snowballs. Show the different snow people they can make. There are two different answers. Show one answer.

4. What if the girls had 13 snowballs, and they made a total of 5 snow people? What would their snow people look like?

5. What if they rolled 15 snowballs, and they made a total of 6 people? What would the snow people look like?

6. What if Kimiko and Tina rolled 15 snowballs, and they made a total of 7 snow people? What would the snow people look like?

7. What if the girls rolled 15 snowballs? Could they make 8 people? Show why or why not.

Underwater School Visitors

Ms. Squid and her school of fish held class in the middle of the ocean. That meant they had lots of visitors swimming by. Sometimes the trumpet fish came by and gave a free concert. Parrot fish and trunkfish swam by every day. All the students looked up from their lessons when the seahorses passed by.

Sometimes a shark would come along. Or an eel would pop its head out of a hole in the nearby rocks to check things out. A giant sea turtle lived beside a large rock in the ocean, and sometimes he would come paddling by. The ray moved quietly and smoothly along the bottom of the ocean.

There were so many visitors that it was hard for the students to work on their lessons. Ms. Squid and her students decided to keep track of all the visitors who came by in one week. They were very surprised to find out how many visitors they had in a week!

NUMBER OF VISITS IN ONE WEEK	
Visitors	Number of Visits
Trumpet Fish	14
Parrot Fish	5
Trunkfish	10
Seahorses	4
Shark	2
Sea Turtle	9
Eel	6
Ray	8

"No wonder this class can't get anything done!" sighed Ms. Squid.

The class decided to make a sign for the school.

**Ms. Squid's
School of Fish**
Quiet, please!
Do NOT disturb.
We have a lot to learn
this year.
Thank you very much!

Underwater School Visitors

Ms. Squid and her students made a bar graph to show how many visitors they had. Complete the graph for them. Use the information from the table on page 44. Then use the graph to answer the questions.

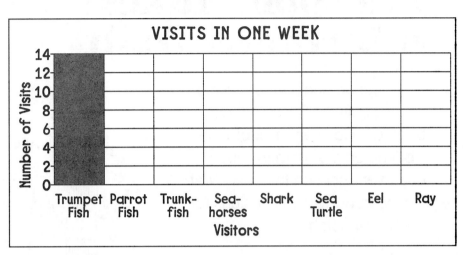

1. Which kind of fish visited the most?

   _____

   How many times did
   this kind of fish visit? _____

2. Which kind of fish visited the least?

   _____

   How many times did
   this kind of fish visit? _____

3. How many more times did the trumpet fish visit than the eel?

   _____

4. How many visits were there from the trunkfish and the sea turtle all together?

   _____

5. How many visits were there from friendly fish all together—trumpet fish, parrot fish, trunkfish, and seahorses?

   _____

6. How many visits were there from less friendly visitors all together—shark, sea turtle, eel, ray?

   _____

7. How many visitors
   were there all together? _____

8. You graphed the visits in **1 week**. About how many visits would there be in **2 weeks** from the following fish?

   parrot fish _____   sea turtle _____

9. About how many visits would there be from the shark in 3 weeks?

   _____

Raccoon Makes a Birthday Quilt

Raccoon decided to make a very special quilt for Snake's tenth birthday. He spent a lot of time working on a pattern to repeat over and over again on the quilt. First Raccoon drew these designs for each quilt patch:

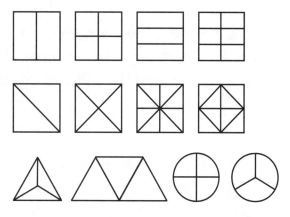

He had to decide which design to use.

Next, Raccoon thought about how he could color the quilt patch. Snake's favorite color was red, so Raccoon decided to use a lot of red.

Last, Raccoon thought about what fraction of the quilt patch he would make red. Would he color the patch $\frac{1}{4}$ red, $\frac{1}{2}$ red, or $\frac{1}{3}$ red?

There were so many things to think about that Raccoon got quite confused.

20 Marvelous Math Tales Scholastic Professional Books

Raccoon Makes a Birthday Quilt

Help Raccoon show the different ways the quilt patch might look.

1. Color $\frac{1}{2}$ of each of these quilt patches red.
   You can use any other colors for the rest of each patch.
   (Make the patch symmetrical if you can.)

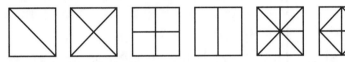

2. Color $\frac{1}{4}$ of each of these quilt patches red.
   You can use any other colors for the rest of each patch.
   (Make the patch symmetrical if you can.)

3. Color $\frac{1}{3}$ of each of these quilt patches red.
   You can use any other colors for the rest of each patch.
   (Make the patch symmetrical if you can.)

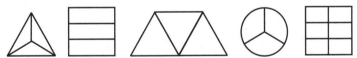

4. Finally, Raccoon decided to use this patch.
   Color the shaded parts red.

The finished quilt is shown below.
Color the shaded parts red.

What fraction of the quilt is red? _____

Name _____

Introducing the Strategy:

Find a Pattern

Sometimes the information in a story problem makes a pattern. Finding that pattern or continuing it may be all you need to do to solve the problem. Look at the story below to see how this strategy works.

Terry Toad could jump high and she could jump far. To make her legs stronger, she practiced jumping all the time. Terry put a number from 1 to 25 on each of the 25 stepping-stones outside her house. First Terry jumped on these numbers: 2, 4, 6, 8, 10, . . .

Do you see the pattern? What would be the next three numbers? They would be 12, 14, and 16 because Terry's jumping on every other stone. She's jumping on the even numbers. No matter how you look at it, Terry's jumping in a pattern!

Next Terry jumped on these numbers: 3, 6, 9, 12, . . .

What are the next three numbers she would jump on? They would be 15, 18, and 21 because Terry's jumping on every third stone. Another way to say it is that she's skipping two stones every time. No matter how you look at it, Terry's jumping in a pattern again!

20 Marvelous Math Tales Scholastic Professional Books

Sally's Patterns

When Sally was a baby, her first words were, "Mama, Dada, Mama, Dada." When she learned to walk, she made a slapping sound with her shoes: "slip, slip, slap, slip, slip, slap." The year that Sally was old enough to clean her room, she put her stuffed animals on her bed in a pattern.

When Sally was a teenager, she got her own phone number. Of course, she made sure the number had a pattern, 323-2323.

When Sally worked at the grocery store in the summer, she made all the displays. She stacked the cereal boxes in a pattern. She piled up the oranges in a pyramid pattern.

Every day Sally followed a pattern. She woke up at the same time, she did her homework at the same time, she watched the same TV shows, and she went to bed at the same time.

Then one day Sally got tired of all the patterns in her life. She put her stuffed animals all over her room. She started waking up at a different time each day. She stacked the cereal boxes in strange ways. Every day was different—and Sally loved it that way!

ORANGES ON SALE $1.50/DOZ.

SOUP SALE!

Sally's Patterns

When Sally was still crazy about patterns, she made lots of them herself. Complete Sally's patterns.

1. ☆ ○ ○ ☆ ○ ○ ☆ ☆ ___ ___ ___

2. **75, 80, 85,** ___ ___ ___

3. ← ↓ ↓ ← ← ↑ ___ ___

4. **A B A A B A A A B** ___ ___

5. **4, 8, 12, 16, 20,** ___ ___ ___

6. □ ⊞ ⊞ ___ ___

7. **3, 8, 13, 18, 23,** ___ ___ ___

8. □ 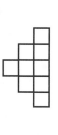 ___ ___

Ms. Dice and the Number Cubes

Danny's class played a lot of games with number cubes. They played games using 6-sided number cubes. They played games using 8-sided number cubes and 12-sided number cubes. They even had a number cube in the shape of a sphere! For teacher appreciation week, the students knew they shouldn't bring flowers or apples to their teacher, Ms. Dice. Each of them brought the most unusual number cube he or she could find.

One day, Ms. Dice took everyone on a trip to a factory where number cubes were made. They watched number cubes with dots on their sides coming off the assembly line.

In the classroom, the students and Ms. Dice studied the 6-sided number cubes they had gotten as gifts from the factory. They were very surprised by all the patterns they found on the number cubes. By the time they were done, the entire class—and Ms. Dice—were number cube experts!

Name _____

Ms. Dice and the Number Cubes

Find some of the patterns that Ms. Dice's class discovered.
You will need two number cubes for the first question
and one number cube for the rest of the questions.

I. Joey looked at the dots on two number cubes to see if the dots on the sides of both of the number cubes are in the same order. Are they?

_____

2. Sara tossed one number cube. She wrote down the top number and the bottom number and added them. Sara kept doing this until she tossed all the possible pairs. Show what Sara got.

_____ + _____ = _____

_____ + _____ = _____

_____ + _____ = _____

_____ + _____ = _____

_____ + _____ = _____

_____ + _____ = _____

3. What pattern do you see?

_____

_____

4. Look again at each pair of numbers. Think about even and odd numbers. What pattern do you see?

_____

_____

_____

5. Ben took one number cube. He put the number 1 on top and the number 4 in front. He turned the cube around, one side at a time, so the 1 was on top, then the 4, then the 6, and then the 3. Try it. Add the four numbers you see on top. What is the sum?

1 + 4 + 6 + 3 = _____

Step I [dice showing 1 on top, 4 in front] **Step 2** [dice showing 6 on top, 3 in front]

6. Then Ben put the number 2 on top and the number 3 in front. He turned the cube around to see four numbers. He added them. What was the sum?

2 + 3 + _____ + _____ = _____

20 Marvelous Math Tales Scholastic Professional Books

Ms. Dice and the Number Cubes

7. Laura started with another number on top. She turned the cube around and added the four numbers she saw. What sum did she get? (Try this. Start with any number on top.)

_____ + _____ + _____ + _____ = _____

8. What pattern do you see?

_____

_____

9. Cut out the number cube and then tape it together. Put the dots in the order they belong. For a challenge, draw the dots on each side before you tape the number cube together.

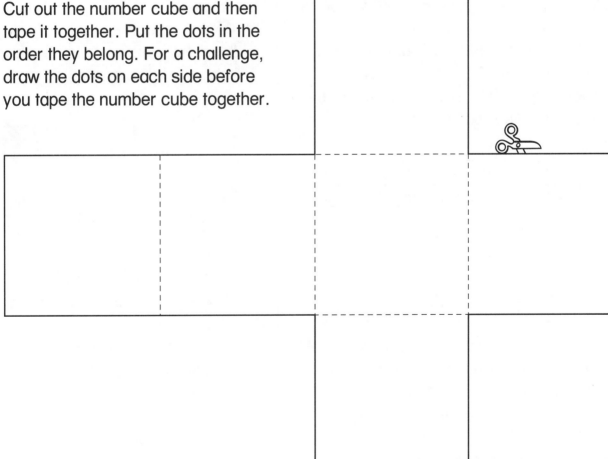

Name _____

Introducing the Strategies:

Make a Table
Make an Organized List

Sometimes the data in a problem are easier to understand if you put them into a table or an organized list. In many cases, the table can help you find a pattern. Here are two examples that show how making a table and making an organized list work.

Make a Table

Nell wanted to learn a lot of Spanish words by the time her Mexican pen pal came to visit. The first week Nell learned 5 new words. The second week she learned 10 new words. The third week Nell learned 15 new words. If this pattern continues, how many new words will she learn in the sixth week?

Nell made a table and looked for a pattern. She saw a pattern in the numbers 5, 10, 15. Those numbers are the numbers you get when you count by fives.

| NUMBER OF SPANISH WORDS LEARNED ||
Week	Number of New Words
1	5
2	10
3	15
4	20
5	25
6	30

Nell also noticed that the number of new words for week 1 was 1 x 5. The number of words for week 2 was 2 x 5, and so on. That was another pattern!

Nell figured out she would learn 30 new words in the sixth week!

Make an Organized List

Carl couldn't decide what to wear one morning. He had a choice of 2 T-shirts and 2 pairs of shorts.

"Maybe I'll try on all the possible outfits," he said. "I wonder how many different outfits there are."

Carl made an organized list to find out how many ways to wear 2 T-shirts and 2 shorts.

"If I wear my baseball shirt, I can wear my white shorts or my black shorts.

"If I wear my striped shirt, I can wear my white shorts or my black shorts."

Carl figured out there were 4 different outfits he could wear. (By the way, he was late to school!)

20 Marvelous Math Tales Scholastic Professional Books

Mr. Pig and His Amazing Machine

Mr. Pig was hungry all the time. When the farmer gave him 1 bucket of corn, Mr. Pig wanted 2 buckets. When the farmer's daughter brought a wheelbarrow of slop, Mr. Pig wanted 2 wheelbarrows. So Mr. Pig decided to build a machine.

He used parts from an old tractor near the pigpen. Day and night, Mr. Pig worked on his amazing machine. He fussed and fussed with the dials on the machine. Nothing happened. Then one day Mr. Pig put 1 old corncob into his machine—and out came 2 corncobs! He was very excited. Every day that week Mr. Pig put in 1 corncob, and every day he got 2 corncobs to eat.

Mr. Pig got to thinking.

"If I put in 2 corncobs at the same time, I wonder what will happen?" he said to himself.

In went 2 corncobs. Out came 4 corncobs. Next Mr. Pig put in 3 corncobs at the same time. How many do you think came out? Mr. Pig had never been so happy in his life!

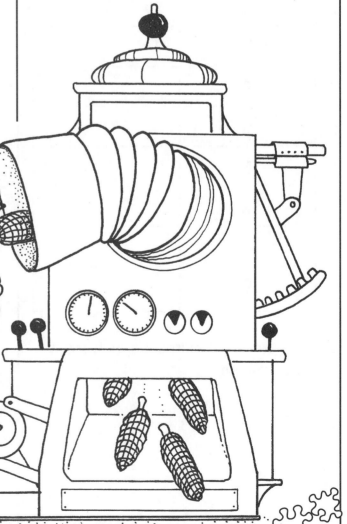

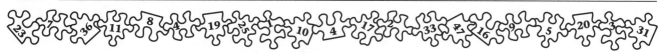

Mr. Pig and His Amazing Machine

Mr. Pig made a table to show what was happening in his machine.

1. What is happening in Mr. Pig's machine? What pattern do you see? Complete the table for Mr. Pig.

Corncobs In	Corncobs Out
1	2
2	4
3	
4	
5	
6	
7	
8	
9	

2. If he puts in 12 corncobs, how many will come out?

_____

3. Then Mr. Pig fussed with the dials. When he put in 1 corncob, 3 corncobs came out! When he put in 2 corncobs, 6 came out! Complete the table.

Corncobs In	Corncobs Out
1	3
2	6
3	
4	
5	
6	
7	
8	
9	

4. If he puts in 12 corncobs, how many corncobs will come out?

_____

What pattern do you see?

_____

20 Marvelous Math Tales   Scholastic Professional Books

Mr. Pig and His Amazing Machine

5. Mr. Pig fussed with the dials again. This time, when he put in 1 corncob, 4 corncobs came out. Complete the table below.

Corncobs In	Corncobs Out
1	4
2	8
3	
4	
5	
6	
7	
8	
9	

6. What pattern do you see?

_____

_____

_____

The next week Mr. Pig fussed with the dials on his machine again. This time when 1 corncob went in, 10 corncobs came out. Mr. Pig thought he would never be hungry again. But when he tried it, the 10 corncobs came flying out of the machine. One hit Mr. Pig on the head. One hit him in the belly. He ducked and tried to get out of the way. That was enough for Mr. Pig. He took apart his machine and politely asked the farmer for seconds whenever he could.

New at the Zoo

Claire was new at the zoo. It was her first job ever, and she was excited. The zookeeper said there were many jobs for Claire to do.

"First there's the job of feeding the lions," said the zookeeper. "They live in the lion house. You feed them raw meat."

Claire swallowed hard. "That sounds kind of—"

"Or you could wash the elephants. They live outside. They get very dusty. The job of feeding and caring for the seals is open, too. You feed the seals by throwing them fish from large buckets."

Claire didn't know which job to take. They all sounded exciting, and they were all so different. Claire decided to make a table to help her decide. She made a table showing the good things and the bad things about caring for each animal. Can you complete the table for her?

Animal	Good Things	Bad Things
lion	beautiful	ferocious
elephant		
seal		smelly fish

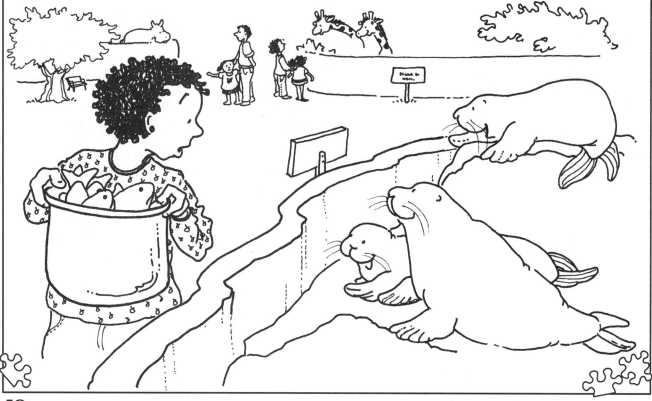

20 Marvelous Math Tales　Scholastic Professional Books

New at the Zoo

Claire asked the zookeeper how much money she would earn every day for each job. Help her figure out how much she would earn.

1. Cleaning elephants: 7 hours
   Earn: $5 for each hour
   How much would she earn in one day?

   Claire would earn _____.

2. Feeding lions: 4 hours
   Earn: $7 for each hour

   Claire would earn _____.

3. Feeding seals: 8 hours
   Earn: $3 for each hour

   Claire would earn _____.

4. Claire made a table to compare how much she would earn for each job. Copy and complete the table.

Animal	Hours	Earned Each Hour	Earned Each Day
elephants	7	$5	$35
lions			
seals			

5. In which job would Claire work the greatest number of hours?

   _____

   In which job would she work the least number of hours?

   _____

6. In which job would Claire earn the greatest amount of money each day?

   _____

   In which job would she earn the least amount money each day?

   _____

7. Which job do you think Claire should take? Tell why.

   _____

   _____

   _____

   _____

23 7 36 11 8 4 19 25 10 4 17 2 33 47 16 9 5 20 3 31

Juan's New Pet

Juan had wanted a pet his whole life. Finally, when he was nine years old, his mother said he was old enough to take care of a pet. That very day, they went to the pound to pick one out. There were rows of cages filled with dogs and cats. Some of the dogs were barking. Some of the animals looked very lonely. It was hard not to want to choose them all.

Juan went to each cage and talked to each animal. The animals loved the attention he gave them. It was a very hard choice. First he had to choose between a cat and a dog. Then he needed to decide if he wanted a young animal or a grown-up animal. Juan could make 4 possible choices for a pet.

young cat
grown-up cat
young dog
grown-up dog

After an hour, Juan decided he wanted a dog—probably a grown-up dog. He had always thought he would get a puppy, but his mom said it was harder for older dogs to find homes. There was one dog that kept smiling at Juan. The dog was a brown, short-haired mutt with a white stripe down its nose. Juan decided to call him Stripe. When the woman in charge let Stripe out of his cage, the dog licked Juan all over his hands and face. They would be pals forever!

Name _____

Juan's New Pet

There were lots of other decisions to make once they got Stripe home. Juan and his mom went to the pet store to get some supplies.

1. Juan wanted to get either a white collar with stars on it or a plain black collar. Then he wanted to get either a white leash or a black leash. Juan can pick one collar and one leash. Draw or write all the different choices for a collar and a leash.

   How many choices are there? _____

2. The dog tags came in different shapes and colors. Draw and color all the possibilities.

   How many choices are there? _____

   | Colors: blue, red, silver |
   | Shapes: ▭ ◯ ♡ |

3. Juan wanted to get 4 toys for Stripe. His mother said he could get 2 toys. Draw a picture or write all the different ways he could pick 2 toys. (There are 6 ways in all.)

ball   bone   stuffed animal   Frisbee

_____   _____

_____   _____

_____   _____

Introducing the Strategy:

Use Logical Reasoning

For some problems, thinking logically and using your head can help you solve them. Here's an example of how this strategy works.

Karla asked her dad how old he was. This is what he said:

> **"My age is between 30 and 39.**
>
> **It's an even number.**
>
> **It's greater than 35.**
>
> **It's not 36.**
>
> **How old am I?"**

Karla used logical reasoning to figure it out. Do steps 2–4 on the number line.

1. She drew a number line starting at 30 and ending at 39.

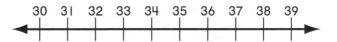

2. She crossed out the odd numbers.

3. She crossed out the numbers 30 to 35.

4. She crossed out 36.

5. She figured out that her dad was 38 years old!

20 Marvelous Math Tales Scholastic Professional Books

Riddling Ronny

Whenever Ronny answered a question, he talked in riddles. His mother tried to get him to stop. His father tried to get him to stop. His brothers and sisters never asked Ronny any questions.

Then one day the cousins came to visit. They asked Ronny how old he was. He said:

"I'm between 3 and 15.
I'm an odd number.
I'm less than 8.
I'm greater than 5."

The cousins tried and tried to figure out how old Ronny was, but they finally gave up.

Then Ronny's uncle asked him how many pets he had. Ronny counted up all his pets and answered:

"I have between 1 and 10.
The number is less than 6.
The number is greater than 2.
The number is not an odd number."

Ronny's uncle tried to figure it out, but he gave up, too.

Name _____

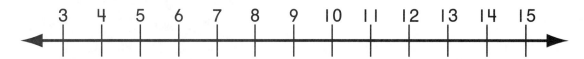

Riddling Ronny

Can you solve Ronny's riddles?

1. How old is Ronny? _____
Use the riddle on page 63 and the
number line below to help you.

3 4 5 6 7 8 9 10 11 12 13 14 15

2. How many pets does Ronny have? _____
Use the riddle on page 63 and the
number line below to help you.

1 2 3 4 5 6 7 8 9 10

3. After all the cousins went home, Ronny asked his
mother how late he could stay up. He reminded her it
wasn't a school night. Ronny's mom thought for a
minute. She decided to give Ronny a taste of his own
riddling. So she answered:

  "It's between 5 and 12.
  It's greater than 8.
  It's less than 12.
  It's an odd number.
  It's not 11."

How late can Ronny stay up? _____ o'clock
Use the riddle above and the
number line below to help you.

5 6 7 8 9 10 11 12

More Riddles from Ronny

Ronny's mother finally got so tired of his riddling that she put her foot down. "That's enough riddling, Ronny. We just can't take it anymore. We need a break. Maybe you can start riddling in a week or two."

Ronny could see she meant what she said. So he answered everyone's questions without riddles. But he wrote down lots of riddles. Ronny decided to save them until he could start telling riddles again.

He made up a riddle about his morning:

"I ate breakfast at 7:00.
I ate lunch at 12:00.
I played baseball 2 hours before I ate lunch.
I cleaned my room 4 hours after I ate breakfast.
What time did I do each activity?"

Ronny solved his own riddle by making a number line with times on it.

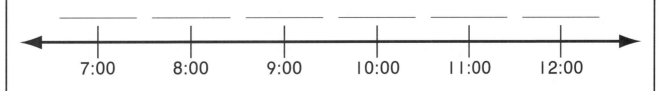

More Riddles from Ronny

1. Can you solve Ronny's riddle on page 65?
   Write in the activities above the times on the number line.
   If there is no activity, leave it blank.

7:00   8:00   9:00   10:00   11:00   12:00

2. Ronny made up this riddle about his afternoon:

"I had dinner at 6:30.
I had a snack 2 hours before dinner. (Be careful.)
I played checkers $\frac{1}{2}$ hour after I had a snack.
I had a sleepover 2 hours after playing checkers.
What time did I do each activity?"

4:30   5:00   5:30   6:00   6:30   7:00

Name _____

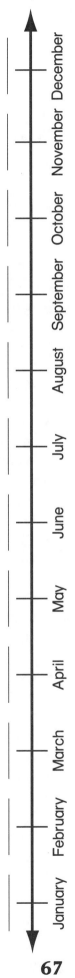

More Riddles from Ronny

3. Here's Ronny's riddle about his week:

"I have piano lessons on Tuesday.
I have drawing class 2 days after my piano lesson.
I have soccer practice between my piano lesson and my drawing class.
I visit my grandpa 3 days before soccer practice.
On what day do I do each activity?"

Sunday   Monday   Tuesday   Wednesday   Thursday   Friday   Saturday

4. Here's Ronny's riddle about his year:

"I got a new baby sister in February.
My birthday was 2 months before we went to the ocean.
We went to the ocean in August.
I learned to ice skate 5 months after I got my baby sister.
I got a new dog between getting a baby sister and my birthday.
I didn't get a new dog in April or May.
What month did each thing happen?"

January February March April May June July August September October November December

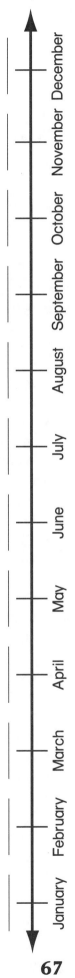

Answers

The Wild Animal Picnic, page 8

Students may circle more words or phrases than indicated, but they must include the information below in their circles.

2. Circled: 17 lions, 18 leopards, 9 jaguars; <u>How many wild cats came to the picnic in all?</u>; 44 wild cats

3. Circled: a total of 23 zebras, 16 zebras; <u>How many zebras played horseshoes?</u>; 7 zebras

4. Circled: 55 mice, 49 rats; <u>How many rodents were there all together?</u>; 104 rodents

5. Circled: 3 monkeys, 9 bananas; <u>how many bananas did they eat in all?</u>; 27 bananas

6. Circled: 59 bees, 76 wasps; <u>How many more wasps came to the picnic than bees?</u>; 17 wasps

7. Circled: 132 sandwiches, 49 sandwiches; <u>How many sandwiches did the lions eat in all?</u>; 181 sandwiches

8. Circled: 145 frogs, 98 toads; <u>What was the total number of frogs and toads in the chorus?</u>; 243 frogs and toads

Froggy's Day at the Store, page 10

2. Add. It costs 55¢ to buy 1 spider and 1 worm. Froggy doesn't want to spend all her money.

3. Add. Two boxes of gnats cost 58¢.

4. Subtract. Froggy needs 3¢ more to buy 2 boxes of gnats.

5. Add. It costs 78¢ to buy 2 worms and 1 cricket.

6. Add. Three worms cost 54¢.

7. Subtract. Froggy will have 1¢ left over if she buys 3 worms.

8. Answers may vary, but should be less than 55¢.

Red Riding Hood and the Gray Wolf, page 12

1. 9 cm, 12 cm, 8 cm; 29 cm

2. 12 cm, 7 cm, 12 cm; 31 cm

3. 7 cm, 11 cm, 8 cm; 26 cm

4. She should take the path by the cave. It's the shortest path.

5. 39 cm

6. 47 cm

7. They should take the path that goes by the fire station because it is the shorter path.

Ms. Squid and the Homework Mess, page 17

1. 5<u>3</u>

2. 4<u>7</u>; <u>3</u>2

3. <u>5</u>4; <u>1</u>4

4. <u>3</u>8

5. <u>1</u>2

6. 2<u>7</u>

7. 3<u>2</u>

8. <u>2</u>6

9. 7<u>9</u>; <u>4</u>2

10. <u>8</u>8

11. <u>5</u>7

12. 8<u>4</u>

Benny's Contests, page 19

1.
```
  76
− 45
  31
```

2. 46

3. Answers may vary. Possible answer is given.
```
  87
− 23
  64
```

4.
```
  96
− 24
  72
```

5.
```
  62
− 49
  13
```

6.
```
  97    greatest
− 56
  41
```

```
  75    least
− 69
   6
```

Jenny's Goofy Calculator, page 21

1. 33	**6.** 32
2. 22	**7.** 27
3. 62	**8.** 23
4. 7	**9.** 27
5. 32	**10.** 67 – 32 = 35

Puzzle Mania, page 23

1. 1 dime, 4 nickels

2. 1 quarter, 3 dimes, 2 pennies

3. 3 quarters, 1 nickel, 1 penny

4. 5 quarters

5. 9 nickels

6. 3 quarters, 2 pennies

7. 3 quarters, 2 dimes, 4 pennies

8. 3 quarters, 1 nickel, 4 pennies

Bumblebee Gets Curious, page 26

1. 4	**10.** 3
2. 4	**11.** 3
3. yes	**12.** no
4. 4	**13.** 5
5. 4	**14.** 5
6. yes	**15.** yes
7. 3	**16.** 8
8. 3	**17.** 8
9. yes	**18.** yes

19. Each shape has the same number of sides as corners.

20. square, rectangle, triangle 1, triangle 2

21. pentagon, octagon

Squirrel's Acorn Problem, page 30

1. 19	**10.** 71
2. 81	**11.** 42
3. 8	**12.** 90
4. 22	**13.** 67
5. 92	**14.** 69
6. 53	**15.** 61
7. 20	**16.** 92
8. 49	**17.** 19
9. 22	**18.** 29

Raccoon Makes a Quilt, page 34

1. Students should draw and identify the following rectangles: $1 \times 12 = 12$ or $12 \times 1 = 12$, $2 \times 6 = 12$ or $6 \times 2 = 12$, $3 \times 4 = 12$ or $4 \times 3 = 12$. Answers may vary. Possible answers: The best quilt would be $1 \times 12 = 12$ because it is long and thin like Snake. The best shape is $3 \times 4 = 12$ because Snake coils up to sleep.

2. Students should draw and identify the following rectangles: $2 \times 12 = 24$ or $12 \times 2 = 24$, $3 \times 8 = 24$ or $8 \times 3 = 24$, $4 \times 6 = 24$ or $6 \times 4 = 24$. Answers may vary. Possible answers: The best quilt is $1 \times 24 = 24$ because it is long and thin like Snake. The best quilt shape is $4 \times 6 = 24$ because Snake coils up to sleep.

What If . . . ?, page 37

1. 2, 0	**7.** 3, 0
2. 2, 2	**8.** 3, 3
3. 3, 0	**9.** 4, 2
4. 4, 0	**10.** 6, 0
5. 6, 0	**11.** 9, 0
6. 12, 0	**12.** 18, 0

Some students may point out that Ken isn't getting any cake or balloons.

Building Snow People, page 42

2.
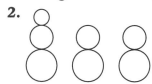

3.
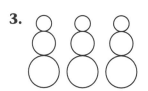

or
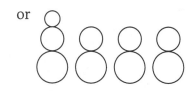

4.
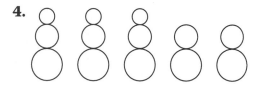

5.
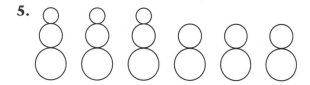

6.

7. Answers may vary. Possible answer: You can't make 8 snow people using 15 snowballs. Tina can make 1 snow person and Kimiko can make 6 snow people out of 15 snowballs for a total of 7 snow people. If you add 1 more snowball, you can't make another snow person.

Underwater School Visitors, page 44

1. trumpet fish, 14
2. shark, 2
3. 8
4. 19
5. 33
6. 25
7. 58
8. parrot fish: 10, sea turtle: 18
9. 6

Raccoon Makes a Birthday Quilt, page 46

1. Answers may vary. Possible answers:

2. Answers may vary. Possible answers:

3. Answers may vary. Possible answers:

4. $\frac{1}{2}$

Sally's Patterns, page 49

1. ○○○☆☆☆○○○○
2. 90, 95, 100, 105, 110, 115, 120, 125
3. ⬇⬅➡⬆⬇⬅➡
4. A A A A B A A A A
5. 24, 28, 32, 36, 40, 44, 48, 52
6. Students should draw a 4 × 4 square and then a 5 × 5 square.
7. 28, 33, 38, 43, 48, 53
8.

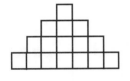 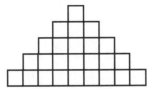

Ms. Dice and the Number Cubes, page 51

1. yes
2. 1 + 6 = 7   4 + 3 = 7
   2 + 5 = 7   5 + 2 = 7
   3 + 4 = 7   6 + 1 = 7
3. When she added the numbers, she always got a sum of 7.
4. There's always an odd number on the top when there's an even number on the bottom, and vice versa.
5. 14
6. 2 + 3 + 5 + 4 = 14
7. Answers may vary, but the sum will always be 14.
8. The sum is always 14.
9. Answers may vary. Possible answer:

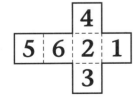 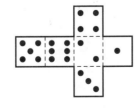

Mr. Pig and His Amazing Machine, page 55

1.

Corncobs In	Corncobs Out
1	2
2	4
3	6
4	8
5	10
6	12
7	14
8	16
9	18

2. 24

3.

Corncobs In	Corncobs Out
1	3
2	6
3	9
4	12
5	15
6	18
7	21
8	24
9	27

4. 36; multiply the number in by 3 to get the number out, or count by 3s.

5.

Corncobs In	Corncobs Out
1	4
2	8
3	12
4	16
5	20
6	24
7	28
8	32
9	36

6. Multiply the number in by 4 to get the number out, or count by 4s.

New at the Zoo, page 58

Answers may vary. Possible answers:

Animal	Good Things	Bad Things
lions	beautiful	ferocious
elephants	lovable	very big and heavy
seals	fun to feed	smelly fish

1. $35
2. $28
3. $24
4.

Animal	Hours	Earned Each Hour	Earned Each Day
elephants	7	$5	$35
lions	4	$7	$28
seals	8	$3	$24

5. seal job, lion job
6. elephant job, seal job
7. Answers may vary. Students may pick the elephant job because the pay is high. Students may pick the lion job because the pay is fairly high and the hours are short. Students may pick the seal job even though the pay is low and the hours are long, because it's the least dangerous.

Juan's New Pet, page 60

1. There are 4 possible choices:
   white collar with stars, white leash
   white collar with stars, black leash
   black collar, white leash
   black collar, black leash

2. There are 9 possible choices:
   blue rectangle   blue heart
   red rectangle   red heart
   silver rectangle   silver heart
   blue circle
   red circle
   silver circle

3. ball and bone
   ball and stuffed animal
   ball and Frisbee
   bone and stuffed animal
   bone and Frisbee
   stuffed animal and Frisbee

Riddling Ronny, page 63

1. 7
2. 4
3. 9

More Riddles from Ronny, page 65

1. 7:00—breakfast
   10:00—baseball
   11:00—cleaned room
   12:00—lunch

2. 4:30—snack
   5:00—checkers
   6:30—dinner
   7:00—sleepover

3. Sunday—Visit Grandpa
   Tuesday—piano
   Wednesday—soccer
   Thurday—drawing

4. February—baby sister
   March—new dog
   June—birthday
   July—ice skating
   August—ocean